Eastside Elementary School
Cleveland ISD
1602 Shell Ave.
Cleveland, TX 77327

Ambulances ✿ Ambulancias

By/Por ERIN FALLIGANT

Illustrated by/Ilustrado por SR. SÁNCHEZ

Music by/Música por MARK OBLINGER

CANTATA
LEARNING

T 1004974

CANTATA
LEARNING

Published by Cantata Learning
1710 Roe Crest Drive
North Mankato, MN 56003
www.cantatalearning.com

Library of Congress Cataloging-in-Publication Data
Names: Falligant, Erin, author. | Sanchez, Sr., 1973– illustrator. |
  Oblinger, Mark, composer. | Falligant, Erin. Ambulances. | Falligant,
  Erin. Ambulances. Spanish.
Title: Ambulances / by Erin Falligant ; illustrated by Sr. Sanchez ; music by
  Mark Oblinger = Ambulancias / por Erin Falligant ; ilustrado por Sr.
  Sanchez ; musica por Mark Oblinger.
Other titles: Ambulancias
Description: North Mankato, MN : Cantata Learning, [2019] | Series: Machines!
  = Las maquinas! | Includes bibliographical references. | Audience: Ages
  6–7. | Audience: Grades K to 3. | English and Spanish.
Identifiers: LCCN 2018026141 (print) | LCCN 2018027119 (ebook) | ISBN
  9781684103560 (eBook) | ISBN 9781684103362 (hardcover) | ISBN
  9781684103720 (pbk.)
Subjects: LCSH: Ambulance service--Juvenile literature. |
  Ambulances--Juvenile literature.
Classification: LCC RA995 (ebook) | LCC RA995 .F35 2019 (print) | DDC
  362.18/8--dc23
LC record available at https://lccn.loc.gov/2018026141

Book design and art direction: Tim Palin Creative
Production assistance: Shawn Biner
Editorial direction: Kellie M. Hultgren
Music direction: Elizabeth Draper
Music arranged and produced by Mark Oblinger

Printed in the United States of America.
0397

ACCESS THE MUSIC!
SCAN CODE WITH MOBILE APP
CANTATALEARNING.COM

TIPS TO SUPPORT LITERACY AT HOME

Daily reading and singing with your child are fun and easy ways to build early literacy and language development.

USING CANTATA LEARNING BOOKS AND SONGS DURING YOUR DAILY STORY TIME

1. As you sing and read, point out the different words on the page that rhyme.

2. Memorize simple rhymes such as Itsy Bitsy Spider and sing them together.

3. Use the critical thinking questions in the back of each book to guide your singing and storytelling.

4. Follow the notes and words in the included sheet music with your child while you listen to the song.

5. Access music by scanning the QR code on each Cantata book. You can also stream or download the music for free to your computer, smartphone, or mobile device.

Devoting time to daily reading shows that you are available for your child. Together, you are building language, literacy, and listening skills.

Have fun reading and singing!

CONSEJOS PARA APOYAR LA ALFABETIZACIÓN EN EL HOGAR

Leer y cantar diariamente con su hijo son maneras divertidas y fáciles de promover la alfabetización temprana y el desarrollo del lenguaje.

USO DE LIBROS Y CANCIONES DE CANTATA DURANTE SU TIEMPO DIARIO DE LECTURA DE CUENTOS

1. Mientras canta y lee, señale las diferentes palabras en la página que riman.

2. Memorice rimas simples como Itsy Bitsy Spider y cántenlas juntos.

3. Use las preguntas críticas para pensar en la parte posterior de cada libro para guiar su canto y relato del cuento.

4. Siga las notas y las palabras en la partitura de música incluida con su hijo mientras escuchan la canción.

5. Acceda la música al escanear el código QR en cada libro de Cantata. Además, puede transmitir o bajar la música gratuitamente a su computadora, teléfono inteligente o dispositivo móvil.

Dedicar tiempo a la lectura diaria muestra que usted está disponible para su hijo. Juntos, están desarrollando el lenguaje, la alfabetización y destrezas de comprensión auditiva.

¡Diviértanse leyendo y cantando!

Ambulances carry people who are hurt or sick to the hospital. You can see and hear an ambulance coming. Its lights flash, and its loud **siren** warns people to get out of the way. Other drivers have to pull over to let ambulances go by. That is the law!

To learn more about ambulances, turn the page and sing along.

Las ambulancias llevan a personas que están lesionadas o enfermas a un hospital. Tú puedes ver y oír a una ambulancia cuando se aproxima. Sus luces destellan y su **sirena** ruidosa alerta a las personas para que se retiren del camino. Otros conductores deben hacerse a un lado para dejar pasar a la ambulancia. ¡Es la ley!

Para aprender más sobre las ambulancias, da vuelta la página y canta la canción.

A car runs off the snowy street
and bumps into a tree.
We stop to dial 9-1-1.
It's an **emergency**!

Un auto se desliza por una calle nevada y choca contra un árbol con fuerza.

Paramos para marcar 9-1-1.

¡Por favor, es una **emergencia**!

The ambulance is on the move.

A-woo! A-woo!

Its lights flash on and off again to get help to us soon!

La ambulancia está por salir.

¡Auuuh, auuuh!

Sus luces destellan una y otra vez,

¡para traernos ayuda con rapidez!

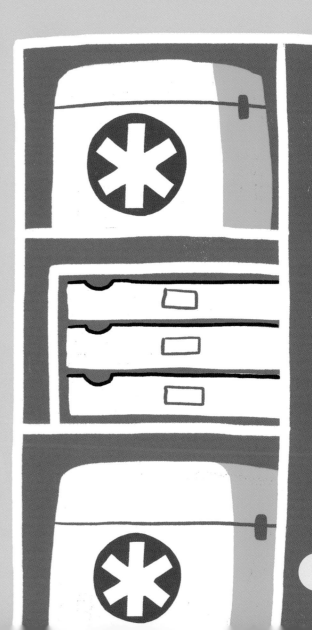

Two big doors open in the back.
There is a bed inside.
A person called an **EMT**
will help out on the ride.

Dos puertas grandes se abren atrás.

Hay una cama en su interior.

Una persona llamada un **EMT**,
ayudará al paciente con su dolor.

The ambulance is on the move.
A-woo! A-woo!
Its lights flash on and off again
to get help to us soon!

La ambulancia está por salir.
¡Auuuh, auuuh!
Sus luces destellan una y otra vez,
¡para traernos ayuda con rapidez!

The hospital is down the street.

The ambulance drives fast.

Woop-woop! Woop-woop! the siren blares.

Honk, honk! Please let us pass!

El hospital está a pocas calles.

La ambulancia conduce rápidamente.

¡Niino, niino!, resuena la sirena.

¡Piiii, piiii! ¡Hazte a un lado totalmente!

The ambulance is on the move.
A-woo! A-woo!
Its lights flash on and off again
to get help to us soon!

La ambulancia está por salir.

¡Auuuh, auuuh!

Sus luces destellan una y otra vez,

¡para traernos ayuda con rapidez!

The ambulance will wait right here
so it can help again.
When someone else calls 9-1-1,
it starts right up and then...

La ambulancia esperará aquí mismo,
para poder ayudar de nuevo.
Cuando alguien más llame al 9-1-1,
encenderá su motor y luego…

The ambulance is on the move.
A-woo! A-woo!
Its lights flash on and off again
to get help to us soon!

La ambulancia está por salir.
¡Auuuh, auuuh!
Sus luces destellan una y otra vez,
¡para traernos ayuda con rapidez!

SONG LYRICS
Ambulances / Ambulancias

A car runs off the snowy street
and bumps into a tree.
We stop to dial 9-1-1.
It's an emergency!

Un auto se desliza por una
 calle nevada
y choca contra un árbol con fuerza.
Paramos para marcar 9-1-1.
¡Por favor, es una emergencia!

The ambulance is on the move.
A-woo! A-woo!
Its lights flash on and off again
to get help to us soon!

La ambulancia está por salir.
¡Auuuh, auuuh!
Sus luces destellan una y otra vez,
¡para traernos ayuda con rapidez!

Two big doors open in the back.
There is a bed inside.
A person called an EMT
will help out on the ride.

Dos puertas grandes se abren atrás.
Hay una cama en su interior.
Una persona llamada un EMT,
ayudará al paciente con su dolor.

The ambulance is on the move.
A-woo! A-woo!
Its lights flash on and off again
to get help to us soon!

La ambulancia está por salir.
¡Auuuh, auuuh!
Sus luces destellan una y otra vez,
¡para traernos ayuda con rapidez!

The hospital is down the street.
The ambulance drives fast.
Woop-woop! Woop-woop! the siren
 blares.
Honk, honk! Please let us pass!

El hospital está a pocas calles.
La ambulancia conduce
 rápidamente.
¡Niino, niino!, resuena la sirena.
¡Piiii, piiii! ¡Hazte a un lado
 totalmente!

The ambulance is on the move.
A-woo! A-woo!
Its lights flash on and off again
to get help to us soon!

La ambulancia está por salir.
¡Auuuh, auuuh!
Sus luces destellan una y otra vez,
¡para traernos ayuda con rapidez!

The ambulance will wait right here
so it can help again.
When someone else calls 9-1-1,
it starts right up and then…

La ambulancia esperará aquí mismo,
para poder ayudar de nuevo.
Cuando alguien más llame al 9-1-1,
encenderá su motor y luego…

The ambulance is on the move.
A-woo! A-woo!
Its lights flash on and off again
to get help to us soon!

La ambulancia está por salir.
¡Auuuh, auuuh!
Sus luces destellan una y otra vez,
¡para traernos ayuda con rapidez!

Ambulances / Ambulancias

Bluegrass
Mark Oblinger

Verse / Verso

1. A car runs off the snow-y street and bumps in-to a tree. We stop to di-al 9-1-1. It's an e-mer-gen-cy! Un au-to se des-li-za por u-na ca-lle ne-va-da y

cho-ca con-tra un ár-bol con fuer-za. Pa-ra-mos pa-ra mar-car nue-ve u-no u-no. ¡Por fa-vor, es un-a e-mer-gen-cia!

Chorus / Estribillo

The am-bu-lance is on the move. A-woo! A-woo! Its lights flash on and off a-gain to get help to us soon! La am-bu-lan-ci-a es-tá por sa-lir. ¡A-

uuuh, a-uuuh! Sus lu-ces des-te-llan u-na y o-tra vez, ¡pa-ra tra-er-nos a-yu-da con ra-pi-dez!

Verse / Verso 2
Two big doors open in the back.
There is a bed inside.
A person called an EMT
will help out on the ride.

Dos puertas grandes se abren atrás.
Hay una cama en su interior.
Una persona llamada un EMT,
ayudará al paciente con su dolor.

Chorus / Estribillo

Verse / Verso 3
The hospital is down the street.
The ambulance drives fast.
Woop-woop! Woop-woop! the siren blares.
Honk, honk! Please let us pass!

El hospital está a pocas calles.
La ambulancia conduce rápidamente.
¡Niino, niino!, resuena la sirena.
¡Piiii, piiii! ¡Hazte a un lado totalmente!

Chorus / Estribillo

Verse / Verso 4
The ambulance will wait right here
so it can help again.
When someone else calls 9-1-1,
it starts right up and then…

La ambulancia esperará aquí mismo,
para poder ayudar de nuevo.
Cuando alguien más llame al 9-1-1,
encenderá su motor y luego…

Chorus / Estribillo

GLOSSARY / GLOSARIO

emergency—when someone is in danger
emergencia—cuando alguien corre
peligro

**EMT (emergency medical
technician)**—a person trained to help
people who are hurt or sick
**EMT (técnico médico de
emergencia)**—una persona entrenada
para ayudar aquellos que están
lesionados o enfermos

siren—equipment that makes a loud
warning sound
sirena—equipo que hace un sonido fuerte
de alerta

CRITICAL THINKING QUESTION

When should you call 9-1-1? Think of an
emergency, when someone should see a doctor
right away. Draw a picture of what happens when
an ambulance arrives to help someone. Then think
of a situation that is *not* an emergency.

PREGUNTA DE PENSAMIENTO CRÍTICO

¿Cuándo deberías llamar al 9-1-1? Piensa en una
emergencia, cuando alguien debería ver a un
doctor enseguida. Haz un dibujo sobre qué sucede
cuando una ambulancia llega para ayudar a
alguien. Luego, piensa en una situación que *no* es
una emergencia.

FURTHER READING / OTROS LIBROS

Bently, Peter. *Ambulance in Action*. London: QEB, 2016.

Bowman, Chris. *Ambulances*. Minneapolis: Bellwether Media, 2018.

Murray, Julie. *Ambulancias*. Minneapolis: Abdo Kids, 2016.

Riggs, Kate. *Ambulances*. Mankato, MN: Creative Company, 2016.

Eastside Elementary School
Cleveland ISD
1602 Shell Ave.
Cleveland, TX 77327